First World War
and Army of Occupation
War Diary
France, Belgium and Germany

15 DIVISION
44 Infantry Brigade,
Brigade Trench Mortar Battery
31 August 1915 - 30 August 1916

WO95/1941/3

The Naval & Military Press Ltd
www.nmarchive.com
Published in association with The National Archives

Published by

The Naval & Military Press Ltd

Unit 10 Ridgewood Industrial Park,

Uckfield, East Sussex,

TN22 5QE England

Tel: +44 (0) 1825 749494

www.naval-military-press.com

www.nmarchive.com

This diary has been reprinted in facsimile from the original. Any imperfections are inevitably reproduced and the quality may fall short of modern type and cartographic standards.

© **Crown Copyright**
Images reproduced by permission of The National Archives, London, England, 2015.

Contents

Document type	Place/Title	Date From	Date To
Heading	Trench Mortar Battery. 1915 Aug-Dec. 1916 Jan. July & Aug. (1916 Feb-June Missing).		
Heading	15 Div 44 Bde 44 Trench Mortar Bty 1915 Aug To 1916 Aug. 1637.		
Heading	NB-1915-Months Confused 1916 Feb-June Missing.		
War Diary		31/08/1915	13/09/1915
War Diary		07/09/1915	29/10/1915
War Diary		15/09/1915	07/12/1915
War Diary		19/11/1915	30/11/1915
Heading	44 Trench Motar Bty Jan 1916. Vol VII.		
War Diary	Belgium B. Series Sheet 28. N.W. I 11 B.	07/01/1916	29/01/1916
Heading	Confidential War Diary of 44th Trench Mortar Battery from 1/7/16 To 31/7/16. (Volume). 15 Div. July. 44.45.46. TMB. Vols.1.		
War Diary	Hohenzollern Sector.	10/07/1916	10/07/1916
War Diary	Right Subsection.	10/07/1916	10/07/1916
War Diary	Left Subsection Seaforth Raid.	10/07/1916	11/07/1916
War Diary	Hohenzollern Sector.	10/07/1916	11/07/1916
War Diary	Right Subsection.	11/07/1916	11/07/1916
War Diary	Left Subsection.	12/07/1916	12/07/1916
War Diary	Right Subsection.	12/07/1916	12/07/1916
War Diary	Left Subsection.		
War Diary	Hohenzollern Sector.	13/07/1916	13/07/1916
War Diary	Right Subsection.	13/07/1916	13/07/1916
War Diary	Left Subsection.		
War Diary	Right Subsection.	14/07/1916	14/07/1916
War Diary	Left Subsection.		
War Diary	Right Subsection.	15/07/1916	15/07/1916
War Diary	Left Subsection.		
War Diary	Hohenzollern Sector.	16/07/1916	16/07/1916
War Diary	Right Subsection.		
War Diary	Left Subsection.	17/06/1916	21/07/1916
War Diary	Noeux.	22/07/1916	23/07/1916
War Diary	Dieval.	24/07/1916	25/07/1916
War Diary	Averdoingt.	26/07/1916	26/07/1916
War Diary	Remeisnil.	27/07/1916	27/07/1916
War Diary	Gezain Court.	28/07/1916	30/07/1916
War Diary	Warnies.	31/07/1916	31/07/1916
Heading	Confidential War Diary of 44th T.M. Battery from 1/8/16 to 31/8/16. (Volume).		
War Diary	Wargnies.	01/08/1916	03/08/1916
War Diary	Miraux.	04/08/1916	04/08/1916
War Diary	Behencourt.	05/08/1916	07/08/1916
War Diary	Albert.	08/08/1916	11/08/1916
War Diary	E.5.B.6.6. Scots Redoobt.	12/08/1916	14/08/1916
War Diary	S.B.3.4.	14/08/1916	17/08/1916
War Diary	S.1.0.5.8. X.6.0.9.1.1/2. X.6.9.9.3.	17/08/1916	17/08/1916
War Diary	S.1.0.3.8.	18/08/1916	23/08/1916
War Diary	X.6.0.3.8.	24/08/1916	28/08/1916
War Diary	E.5.B.6.6.	29/08/1916	29/08/1916

War Diary   E.8.A.76.   30/08/1916   30/08/1916

1941/3   TRENCH MORTAR
         BATTERY.

1915   AUG - DEC
1916   JAN
       JULY + AUG.

(1916 Feb - June missing!)

~~2 Army Troops~~

15 DIV 44 Bde

44

TRENCH MORTAR
BTY

1915 AUG — 1916 AUG

(1637)

NB -
1915 -
Months
confused

1916
Feb - June
missing

WAR DIARY
or
INTELLIGENCE SUMMARY.

(Erase heading not required.)

Army Form C. 2118.

Instructions regarding War Diaries and Intelligence Summaries are contained in F. S. Regs., Part II. and the Staff Manual respectively. Title pages will be prepared in manuscript.

Place	Date	Hour	Summary of Events and Information	Remarks and references to Appendices
	1915			
	31 Aug		This battery was formed at the Grand Horringer School, and Lieut. C.D.S. Evans R.G.A. took over command of same	
	1st Sept	9 a.m.	Battery drill	
	2nd "	9 a.m.	Battery drill	
	3rd "	8 p.m.	Lieut. J. Hansen R.F.A. attached for duty	
	4th "	9 a.m.	Battery drill	
	5th "	2.30 p.m.	Battery proceeded from Bustar to Headquarters 3rd Nott Midland Brigade Ammunition Column, Barcelona	
		5 p.m.	Reported arrival of battery to C.R.A. 46th Division and was informed that Battery was to be attached to 138th Infantry Brigade. Orders received from C.R.A. 46th Division to send 1st & 2nd gun detachments to the 29th Battery and 1 & 2nd gun stores to review points to the 113th Battery	
	6th "	11 a.m.	Reported to Brigade Major 138th Infantry Brigade, and proceeded to the trenches and reported to the Commanding Officers of the 4th and 5th Lincolns	
		9 p.m.	Gun detachments brought into trenches. Two 1½ inch guns and stores were taken over from the O.C. 43rd Battery with 17 rounds of light bombs	

Army Form C. 2118

WAR DIARY
or
INTELLIGENCE SUMMARY.
(Erase heading not required.)

Instructions regarding War Diaries and Intelligence Summaries are contained in F. S. Regs., Part II. and the Staff Manual respectively. Title pages will be prepared in manuscript.

Place	Date	Hour	Summary of Events and Information	Remarks and references to Appendices
	8th Sept.		Situation quiet. Nothing to report.	
	9th Sept		Two new gun positions chosen. One for 6 in gun and one for 4.7 in gun	
	10th Sept		Work commenced on new positions	
	11th Sept	10 pm	German T.M. fired into Trench 52. Replied on mor and wire cutting posts of 11th R.I.R's. Fire 5 rounds of 2 inch. Find two dud to explode (March 97 fh impr mor). Remaining three successful (March 96 fuze inst). The 2.8 in mor fired 16 rounds in afternoon at enemy's	
	12 Sept		Work continued on gun emplacements. Hindered in afternoon by aeroplanes continually flying overhead	
	13 Sept		Continued work on gun emplacements and shot new dug out behind mess at position. Bed of 2 in gun placed in position. On 6 in. and one 2.7 in. cartridge sent to enlarge French Pistrian Comm. and Sentences met. By order of Bgd D.F. Continued work on emplacements and dug out. Dug out finished	
		1.30	Relief party leaves	

WAR DIARY or INTELLIGENCE SUMMARY.

Army Form C. 2118.

Place	Date	Hour	Summary of Events and Information	Remarks and references to Appendices
1st	7 Sept		Positions chosen for two guns.	
	8th		Began building official dug out also areas.	
	9th		Two guns placed in position.	
	10th		Last gun placed in position.	
	11th		Officers dug out finished also areas.	
			Fired three rounds of 2 inch in reply to "Enemy's last failed to explode. Enemy replies with about 30 H.E. shells. Bomb store fired for 2" gun in Armagh Wood.	K 2/15/15
	12.		Fired bounds light 1½ inch from Trench 48, at 140 yds, three bursts in 14 air & three before correctly. Enemy replies with about 5 rounds. Dug out begun for men in Trench 41; also bomb-store. Enemy bombarded trenches. 4 & 50 heavy between 3.30 & 5 p.m.	
	13.		Dug out & bomb store in 41 finished. Enemy bombarded trenches on three occasions, each lasting for 1¼ hrs.	
	14.		Dug out & bomb store begun near 2" gun in assembly trench behind junction of 49 & 50.	

A.F. Silvan Lieut R.G.A.
O.C. 144th Trench Howitzer Battery

Army Form C. 2118

WAR DIARY
or
INTELLIGENCE SUMMARY.
(Erase heading not required.)

Instructions regarding War Diaries and Intelligence Summaries are contained in F.S. Regs., Part II. and the Staff Manual respectively. Title pages will be prepared in manuscript.

Place	Date	Hour	Summary of Events and Information	Remarks and references to Appendices
	16 Sept.		Aug-at began for many hours in communication trench behind trench 50.	
	16 Sept.		Bay-at in trench 50 finished.	
	17 Sept.		Enemy bombarded trenches heavily for 2 hours.	
	18 Sept.		Situation normal. Artillery to support.	
	19th Sept.		Situation normal. German bombarded Hooge trench at 6 p.m. Servants dug out. began	
	20 Sept.		Fired 5 18pr. rounds from trench 41 in reply to about a dozen rifle grenades be burst in air and three failed to explode.	
	21st Sept.		We bombarded Hooge at 5.30 a.m. Parapet round 2 inch guns in through March organised. Servants dug out finished.	
	22nd Sept.		Parapet round 2 inch gun finished. British close for 2 inch gun in desired communication trench from end of 475 trenches Zillebeke.	
	23 Sept.		Situation normal. Artillery to front.	
	24 Sept.		Situation normal. Artillery to front.	
	25 Sept 3.50 am		English bombarded Hooge trench at 3.50 a.m. No particular bombardment continued for 2 hour in original intensity. Bombardment spread to our line, and artillery went on for 2 hour.	

WAR DIARY or INTELLIGENCE SUMMARY

Army Form C. 2118

(Erase heading not required.)

Place	Date	Hour	Summary of Events and Information	Remarks and references to Appendices
	25th Sept.		Bursts of shelling during afternoon and evening. No work could be done.	
	26th Sept.	3.30am	Germans bombarded our lines for a short time at 3.20 am and again on the entering.	
		10.10pm	Opened up with fire at Stroppe station like bombarding.	
	27th Sept.		Continues shelled defensive position for 2nd day on through wood inspected. Whizz-bangs at intervals during the day.	
	28th Sept.		Situation Quiet. Received 18 light bombs and 16 heavy.	
	29th Sept.		Mine blown up by the Germans, followed by rapid rifle fire.	
	30th Sept.	7pm	German flare up of a shine in trench 47. This was followed by strong burst and rapid rifle fire. Fired 3 3.30pm bombs and 2 18pr bombs all expended correctly.	
	1st Oct.		German shew up a ?? Quiet sunday. Fired no.	
	2nd Oct.		Quiet. Nothing to report.	
	3rd Oct.		Quiet. Nothing to report.	
	4th Oct.		Situation Quiet. Nothing to report.	
	5th Oct.		Situation Quiet. Nothing to report.	
	6th Oct.		Situation Quiet. Nothing to report. Lieut. M. Osprey 3rd Battn East Kent Regt. joined for duty.	
	7th Oct.		Situation Quiet. Nothing to report.	

G.F. Sloan, Lieut. R.G.A.
O.C. A 4. Heavy Mortar Battery

WAR DIARY or INTELLIGENCE SUMMARY
Army Form C. 2118

Place	Date	Hour	Summary of Events and Information	Remarks and references to Appendices
	Oct 23		German shelling from Zobeck in the afternoon till six 5 in hrs. and 13 hy. how high explosive shell	
	24		Nothing to report.	
	25	9 p.m.	The cooks that were relieved from the trenches, limbers, guns and ammunition were shelled. One wagon shot in a shell hole for 1½ hours. One 15 inch gun off at B.22 Central. Continued to H.29.C.62.	
	26	8 a.m.	ammunition & a.m. Nothing to report. Further reconnoitred. off for trenches at 5 p.m. till has 2nd Guns	
	27		Began work into a round position behind T.1 trench in case of need but all need has been put started under bad weather conditions by fatigue parties from the infantry. There was great difficulty in getting guns and ammunition along trenches from Ry. to T.1 owing to then the knee deep mud plus. It a disgraceful condition. An hour and a half was taken to get the gun into place into required spot.	
	28		Gun placed in newly dug gun pit. Registration or new crater and lamp crater started T.1 carried out at 13 h.m. the rounds fired. Fire rounds fired into new craters about 7 h.m. This crater was supposed to be strongly held by German bombers parties. Three out of total 8 rounds fired were duds. Sent 5 rounds into in crater. Reliefs place	

Lieutenant 1/1 the B. of B. 4/7 R. Scots.

Army Form C. 2118.

WAR DIARY
or
INTELLIGENCE SUMMARY.
(Erase heading not required.)

Instructions regarding War Diaries and Intelligence Summaries are contained in F. S. Regs., Part II. and the Staff Manual respectively. Title pages will be prepared in manuscript.

Place	Date	Hour	Summary of Events and Information	Remarks and references to Appendices
	15 Sept.		Sheikhi Zowaid. Nothing to report.	
	16 Sept.		Dug out for men completed in Stand 49.	
	17 Sept.		Sheikhi Zowaid. nothing to report.	
	18 Sept.		Sheikhi Zowaid. nothing to report.	
	19 Sept.	7.30 a.m	Fired three bombs in reply to enemy's heavy mortar. First two successful, but no burst air high.	
	19 Sept.	3 p.m	Fired two bombs in reply to enemy's heavy mortar. One burst correctly, the other failed to explode.	
	20 Sept.	3 p.m	Enemy shelled the back of Stand 49.	
	21 Sept.	6.30 p.m	Enemy shelled around here and the back of Stand 49.	
		8.3 p.m	Relief took place.	

JR 21/9/15

C. F. Silman. Lieut R.G.A.
O.C. 44th Heavy Howitzer Battery

Army Form C. 2118.

WAR DIARY
or
INTELLIGENCE SUMMARY.
(Erase heading not required.)

Instructions regarding War Diaries and Intelligence Summaries are contained in F. S. Regs., Part II. and the Staff Manual respectively. Title pages will be prepared in manuscript.

Place	Date	Hour	Summary of Events and Information	Remarks and references to Appendices
	30 Sept.		Bomb throw built and gun emplacement finished.	
		9 p.m.	Infantry took their stations in front of trench T.1. Enemy made three bombing attacks but were repulsed.	
	31 Sept / 1st Oct.		Situation normal. Nothing to report.	
	2nd Oct / 3rd Oct.		Situation normal. Nothing to report. Gun emplacement and look slits in T.7 fell in owing to wet weather.	
			Situation normal. Artillery stopped. Brand new emplacement and whiz-bang, also whiff-bang. Enemy whiz-banged us at intervals during the day. Gun emplacement in T.7 flooded out. Re. Brand another batteries desired us and said we were to take the gun out of action, and to build fresh gun emplacement.	
	4th Oct.		Situation normal. Nothing to report. Relief took place.	

JK 7/10/1

C.P. Schwarz
Lieut. R.G.A.
OC. 4.4" Flint Howitzer Battery.

Army Form C. 2118

44th Trench Mortar Battery

WAR DIARY
or
INTELLIGENCE SUMMARY

(Erase heading not required.)

Place	Date	Hour	Summary of Events and Information	Remarks and references to Appendices
	5/11		Commenced building dugout. Guides of wire in old dug out impossible to remove. Weather fine. Situation normal.	
	6/11		Dugout continued. One 2 inch and one 6 in. of fallen in emplacement. Situation normal.	
	7/11		Few emplacement built behind T1. Some shelling on R1 & R5 = 250/15	
	8/11		Work for about three hours.	
	9/11		Emplacement behind R2 continued. Weather dull. Registration evening. Situation normal.	
	10/11		Work on T1 emplacement and dugout. Situation normal.	
	11/11		Work at T1 emplacement. Relief taken place. Situation normal. Weather wet.	

J.W. [signature]
OC 44 Trench Mortar Battery

Army Form C. 2118.

WAR DIARY
INTELLIGENCE SUMMARY.
(Erase heading not required.)

Instructions regarding War Diaries and Intelligence Summaries are contained in F. S. Regs., Part II. and the Staff Manual respectively. Title pages will be prepared in manuscript.

Place	Date	Hour	Summary of Events and Information	Remarks and references to Appendices
	12th Nov.		Situation Quiet nothing to report.	
	13th Nov.		Situation Quiet nothing to report. Two new gun positions chosen.	
	14th Nov.		Gun emplacement built for 1½ inch gun in trench G2.	
	15th Nov.		Situation Quiet nothing to report.	
	16th Nov.		Gun emplacement built for 1inch gun in trench T.7.	
	17th Nov.		Bomb store started in trench T.7.	Mens dug out enlarged in trench G2.
	18th Nov.		Mens dug out started in trench T.7. Relief takes place.	

C.R. Shram Lieut. R.G.A.
O.C. 44th Trench Mortar Battery.

Army Form C. 2118.

WAR DIARY
or
INTELLIGENCE SUMMARY.
(Erase heading not required.)

1/4th French Mortar Battery

Place	Date	Hour	Summary of Events and Information	Remarks and references to Appendices
	1 Dec.		Breakfasts 8-0. Inspection 9.30. Physical drill 10-0 to 11-0. Inspection 82. Reflare 11-30 to 12-30. Dinners 12-45. 2-0 to 30. Squad Drill, Rounds of butts service for bullets 5-30	
	2 Dec.		Breakfasts 8-0. Inspection 9-30. 10 – 7:30 Route march 10 to 12-30. Dinners 12 to 12-45. Semaphore 2-0.	
	3 Dec.		Breakfasts 8-0. Inspection 9-30. Physical drill 10-11. Reflare instruction 11-30 to 12-30. Dinners 12-45. Squad drill 2 to 3. Heavy Rain.	
	4 Dec.		Breakfast 8-0. Inspection 9-30. Physical drill 10-11. Semaphore 11-30 to 12-30. Dinners 12-45. Squad drill 2 to 3. Heavy Rain.	
	5 Dec.		8-0 Breakfasts. 10-0 Church Parade for R.C.; Short statement for remainder.	
	6 Dec.		Breakfasts 8-0. Physical Drill 10-11. Instruction in Semaphore 11-30-12.30. Parades for night cancelled owing to wet weather, and men made to clean up kit and shoes etc.	
	7 Dec.		8-0 Breakfasts 9-30. Inspection of Rifles 10 to 11. Squad drill 11-30 to 12.30. Instruction in Reflare 2 to 3. Men paraded for kit inspection.	

W.J. McGuire

WAR DIARY
or
INTELLIGENCE SUMMARY.
(Erase heading not required.)

Army Form C. 2118.

Place	Date	Hour	Summary of Events and Information	Remarks and references to Appendices
	19/10/15		Drained gun position behind T.1. Also water drained from outside horse dugouts. Weather fine.	
	20.10.15		New hangar bomb store commenced behind T.1. Found ground very difficult to drain as that of T. Bomb store continued. Drainage of mens dug outs continued. Weather fine.	
	21.10.15		Bomb store finished. Weather fine.	
	22.10.15		All stores reclassified and cleaned. Gun hooters, sights, oiled weather Fine	
	23.10.15		Relief to the plus 24th Batt. taking over all stores, guns, ammo, guns bombs etc. togethy	
	24.10.15		half of Batterys proceeds to watten. Remainder stayns, or Reningalst. Battery stores sent with togeths. Fully.	
	25.10.15		Remainder ½ of Battery at Reningelst proceeded with the 15/5/1915 A.C. and proceeds with the to Steenvoorde. Ratin drawn from 107 BAC.	
	26.10.15		Rest at Steenvoorde.	
	27.10.15		Proceed from Steenvoorde to Rubrock. Billets found there for tonight.	
	28.10.15		Proceed from Rubrock to Acquin where Billets in to be allotted billeted for rest and winter trainings. Ratins drawn from 107 BAC.	
	29.10.15		Men prestent, as all went on 16 hour travelling on 28 inst.	
	30.10.15		Semaphore and physical drill parades	

H. Spearpoint,
Major

4.4 Trench Mortar Bty
Jan 916
Vol VII

Army Form C. 2118.

44th Trench Mortar School

WAR DIARY
INTELLIGENCE SUMMARY.
(Erase heading not required.)

Instructions regarding War Diaries and Intelligence Summaries are contained in F. S. Regs., Part II. and the Staff Manual respectively. Title pages will be prepared in manuscript.

Place	Date	Hour	Summary of Events and Information	Remarks and references to Appendices
Belgium B. Sheet. 28. N.W. I 11 R.	7 Jan		Took over area covered by the 32nd Trench Mortar Battery 7th Division.	
	8th "		Slow. Gun positions checked stores. Guns in action three 2inch guns.	
	9th "	3:30 p.m.	Cleaned guns & stores. Limited on 2nd gun ϕ out of action owing to emplacement being flooded out. Fired Jan 2 2nd bombs at enemy front line in reply to light trench mortars. Continued building new dug out.	
	10th "		Situation normal.	
	11th "		Situation normal. Cleaned guns & stores. Continued building new dug out.	
	12th "	2:30 p.m.	Fired eight 2inch bombs in reply to enemy light trench mortars.	
	13th "		Situation normal.	
	14th "		Situation normal. Relief took place.	

[Signed]
W. Brown, Lieut. R.G.A.
O.C. 44th Trench Mortar Battery.

WAR DIARY
INTELLIGENCE SUMMARY

(Erase heading not required.)

Army Form C. 2118.

Place	Date	Hour	Summary of Events and Information	Remarks and references to Appendices
Belgium B Series Sheet 28 NW T.11.6	15/1/16		Situation normal. Fatigues on wires dugouts cleaning ammunition	
	16.1.16		" normal.	
	17.1.16	3.30 pm	Three rounds fired by A and C guns to test ranges. Fatigues on dugouts.	
	18.1.16	4 pm	Two hostile planes fired to put a stop to continuous bombing from German craters, 20 alarming	
		8.40 pm	were done by their bombs, heard all falling short of our parapet.	
	19.1.16	8.45	Four expended on A.P. What was our air front bursting about 3 yards above the parapet. It	
		12.0 midnt	impossible to get at either of our guns. Fatigues on dugouts cumular after shell	
			H/S 17, 18, 19 and 20 heavily shelled by 5.9 cm & Howitzers	
	20.1.16	8.30 pm	Fatigues carried out on dugouts cleaning and purifying of ammunition &c	
			Rapid fire. Alban trifle of the enemy. All and Bessel wounded	
	21.1.16		Fatigues thermal. Situation thermal.	
			Enemy trench mortar mind forward for 120 lb and shells about 800 rounds fired to	
	22.1.15		Enemy. Also a good many small shells about 8 lbs and 4 inch shrapnel were fired at a very rapid rate. All the fire to explode our two end bombs were fired by no less	

Army Form C. 2118.

WAR DIARY
INTELLIGENCE SUMMARY
(Erase heading not required.)

Place	Date	Hour	Summary of Events and Information	Remarks and references to Appendices
Belgium. B. Sere. Sheet 28. N.W. I.11.b.	2nd Jan.		Situation normal. Cleaned guns and stores.	
	24th "	11 a.m.	Fired two 2 inch bombs at enemy's front line in reply to trench mortars.	
	25th "	2.30 p.m.	Fired three 2 inch bombs at enemy's front line in reply to heavy trench mortars. (120 lb. shell) No damage was done by their bombs.	
	26th "		Situation normal. Built reserve trench store behind H.20.	
	27th "		Situation normal. Fatigues on new dug out.	
	28th "		Situation normal. Selected position for 1½ inch gun behind trench H.20.	
	29th "	3 p.m.	Fired five 3.7 inch bombs at enemy machine gun emplacement. Emplacement apparently damaged.	
		3.10 p.m.	Fired five 3.7 inch bombs at enemy working parties near machine gun emplacement.	
		6.30 p.m.	Fired five 3.7 inch bombs into crater opposite trench H.20 in reply to enemy's rifle grenades.	
			Three Trench Mortars in crater.	
		7 p.m.	Relief took place.	

C.P. Sherran. Lieut. R.F.A.
O.C. 44th Trench Mortar Battery.

1st Div. July

44
45 } T M B
46 } V&Ls 1

Confidential

War Diary
of
44th Trench Mortar Battery.

from 1/7/16 to 31/7/16.

(Volume)

Army Form C. 2118

WAR DIARY
or
INTELLIGENCE SUMMARY
(Erase heading not required.)

44th L.M. Battery

Place	Date.	Hour	Summary of Events and Information	Remarks and references to Appendices
HOHENZOLLERN SECTOR Right Subsection	10.7.16		No 2 gun was trained on some snipers' plates opposite ALEXANDER Sap. 12 rounds were fired altogether, from observation the fire was good but not so far as could be observed successful in destroying snipers.	
Left Subsection SEAFORTH RAID	10/11		In this raid the Stokes guns took part both on the right and on the left front where the raid took place. The bombardment on the right was merely to draw the enemy's attention from the actual spot of attack. On the right 160 rounds were fired. On the immediate front of attack the Stokes guns was to silence enemy machine gun at G.4.B.3.9 ; G.4.B.3.1½ also support emp at G.4.B.7.7. 4" Stokes guns were also used on this occasion to put a smoke barrage in front of enemy machine gun emplacements.	
		11.30pm	At zero hour 11.30pm in cooperation with artillery the Stokes guns commenced firing at the machine guns which had been allotted to them. In all 303 3" shells were fired with marked success for practically no enemy machine guns were heard to fire. The four M.G. stokes fired over 24 smoke shells.	

WAR DIARY or INTELLIGENCE SUMMARY

Army Form C. 2118

Place	Date	Hour	Summary of Events and Information	Remarks and references to Appendices
HOHENZOLLERN SECTOR.	10/11		Seaforth road Crater. One gun only right subsection out of one gun on the left subsection was knocked out during the bombardment.	
right subsection	11/16	11am	No 1 gun fired during artillery bombardment at 1 pm. Twenty rounds were fired of which 10 rounds were observed to land in enemy's sap. No 2 gun also took part in this strafe firing 22 rounds. This gun was later shifted from CROWN TRENCH to DRUMMOND TRENCH.	
left subsection			After the firing was chiefly in retaliation. 52 rounds were fired.	
right subsection	12/16	2.30am	No 1 gun cooperated with artillery at 2.30 pm. and again at 4.30 pm. The fire in these sessions was slow and deliberate the gun being traversed after each shot. No of rounds fired 20. No 2 gun at 7.15 pm in cooperation with "D Coy 8/10 GORDONS" who were firing rifle grenades sent over 20 rounds along enemy front line between G.S.C.1,2.3½ and G.S.C.1½.4½. The shooting was decidedly good.	
Left Subsection			Mort firing was chiefly in retaliation to enemy darts. In practically every case the enemy's fire was stopped. Forty nine rounds were fired.	

Army Form C. 2118

WAR DIARY
or
INTELLIGENCE SUMMARY
(Erase heading not required.)

Instructions regarding War Diaries and Intelligence Summaries are contained in F. S. Regs., Part II. and the Staff Manual respectively. Title Pages will be prepared in manuscript.

Place	Date	Hour	Summary of Events and Information	Remarks and references to Appendices
HOHENZOLLERN SECTOR	13/7/16	3.10p		
Right subsection			No.1 gun retaliated on enemy front line behind HAIRPIN CRATERS. Soon after firing had ceased an enemy aerial dart landed in the emplacement and knocked the gun out. Twenty one rounds fired.	
		3.5p	No.2 gun opened fire on enemy trenches at G.5.c.1½.3½ in a line of werdung ramp. Six hits on enemy parapet were obtained. Enemy much less active than previously. 44 rounds fired.	
Left subsection	14/7/16		Intermittent firing throughout the day.	
Right subsection		9.45p	We strafed behind CRATER at G.5.c.2½.7. Some good shrapnel effects were observed. Rounds fired 32.	
Left subsection	15/7/16		52 rounds fired in retaliation to enemy darts etc.	
			Hand at T.M. suspected at G.5.c.3½.7½ which was silenced and was not again fired. Intermittent firing throughout the day. Rounds fired 52.	
Left subsection			Special attention was paid throughout the day to enemy dart battery at G.4.B.4.3½ which was silenced. Rounds fired 45.	

Army Form C. 2118

WAR DIARY
or
INTELLIGENCE SUMMARY
(Erase heading not required.)

Instructions regarding War Diaries and Intelligence Summaries are contained in F.S. Regs., Part II. and the Staff Manual respectively. Title Pages will be prepared in manuscript.

Place	Date	Hour	Summary of Events and Information	Remarks and references to Appendices
HOHENZOLLERN SECTOR Right Subsection	16/7		Guns very active during 24 hrs. 130 rounds being fired. Guns fired at enemy fifteen minutes amidst our guns the night in enemy war.	
Left "	17/7		Intermittent firing during day and night. 76 rounds fired. Very little firing all day. Any firing was in retaliation.	
	18/7		Right Guns fired 168 rounds attending trenches onwards at G.5.c.2.3½ and G.5.c.5½.2½. Traversing along enemy front line. No 1 gun fired 74 rounds behind new crater at G.5.c.9½.1. effect good.	
	19/7		Right gun fired 138 rounds in reventing and bombar chment of enemy front line at G.5.c.2.3½.	
	20/7		Very quiet all day. Little or no firing done.	
	21/7		Battery relieved by 25th T.M. Battery in accordance with 44 T.R. 0066	

Army Form C. 2118

WAR DIARY
or
INTELLIGENCE SUMMARY
(Erase heading not required.)

Instructions regarding War Diaries and Intelligence Summaries are contained in F.S. Regs., Part II. and the Staff Manual respectively. Title Pages will be prepared in manuscript.

Place	Date	Hour	Summary of Events and Information	Remarks and references to Appendices
NOEUX.	22/7		Battery marched to NOEUX and billetted there over night. 22/23.	
	23/7		Battery marched to DIEVAL in accordance with 44 D/3. 0067. On the occasion the walking wore along with them 240 horses in half sects. No men fell out.	
DIEVAL	24/7		Battery did training in open fighting	
	25/7		Training carried out as on previous day.	
OVERDOINGT	26/7		Battery marched to OVERDOINGT in accordance with 44 D/3. 0068.	
REMAISNIL	27/7		Battery marched to REMAISNIL in accordance with 44 D/3. 0069.	
GEZAINCOURT	28/7		Battery marched to GEZAINCOURT in accordance with 44 D/3. BM 635.	
	29/7		Training in wood fighting	
	30/7		Training in wood fighting continued.	
WARGNIES.	31st		In accordance with 44 D/3. 0070. Battery moved to WARGNIES.	

M.W. Thorn Capt.
O.C. E. Bat.

Confidential

War Diary

of

44" T. M. Battery

from 1/8/16
to 31/8/16.

(Volume).

Army Form C. 2118.

24th Light Trench Mortar Battery

WAR DIARY
or
INTELLIGENCE SUMMARY.
(Erase heading not required.)

Instructions regarding War Diaries and Intelligence Summaries are contained in F. S. Regs., Part II. and the Staff Manual respectively. Title pages will be prepared in manuscript.

Place	Date	Hour	Summary of Events and Information	Remarks and references to Appendices
WARGNIES	1st Sep		The Battery practiced digging themselves in, & fishing etc	
"	2nd		The day was devoted to advancing thro' woods, passing obstacles etc	
"	3rd		Gun Pit digging & ammunition pits building were carried out	
MIRAUX	4th		In accordance with 24th Inf Brigade O.O. 71, the Battery marched to MIRAUX & billetted there.	
BEHENCOURT	5th		In accordance with 24th Inf Brigade O.O. 72, the Battery moved into billets at BEHENCOURT.	
"	6th		The Battery paraded for Divine Service & afterwards in Battery formation	
"	7th		Gun drill & Gun emplacement digging	
ALBERT	8th		In accordance with 24th Inf Brigade O.O. 73, the battery marched to ALBERT & relieved the 68th L.T.M. By in reserve	
"	9th		In reserve. Gun drill &	
"	10th		do do	
"	11th		Infantry drill &	
"	12th		do do	
E.5.B.6.6 SCOTSREDOUBT	13th		In accordance with 24th Inf Brigade O.O. the Battery moved to pt E.5.B.6.6.	
"	14th		In accordance with 24th Brigade BM 962 the Battery moved to SCOTS REDOUBT	
			Relieved 45 T.M. By in line in accordance with 24th I.B. O.O. 74. during	

WAR DIARY or INTELLIGENCE SUMMARY

Army Form C. 2118.

(Erase heading not required.)

Instructions regarding War Diaries and Intelligence Summaries are contained in F. S. Regs., Part II. and the Staff Manual respectively. Title pages will be prepared in manuscript.

Place	Date	Hour	Summary of Events and Information	Remarks and references to Appendices
S.0.3.4	12th		During the day we had a considerable number of rounds intermittently aimed at S.8.3.4 in order to make any of the enemy in that trench show themselves. Snipers worked in cooperation. Quite a number of Germans were killed.	
	13th		We had a few rounds pro that all day but the enemy of the 8th Div. were very busy shooting them.	
	16th		During the day we had slight activity and same.	
	17th		In afternoon and night the enemy C.O. 75 lm was shelled slightly at targets at C.O. 75 lm did not target D.	
S.10.58 X.6.0.9.1½ X.6.9.9.3		8.55am	S.10.58 and about X.6.9.1½ to X.6.9.9.3 during the Bosch shelled D. fired time. Zero hour was 8.55 am & at that time we fired for 1 minute on X.6.0.9.1½ to X.6.0.9.3 with two guns firing on all about 30 rounds.	
			On that we observed to fall in a well with the time went from us by some red very light shots. They been no rather rifle fire & rifle a/c.	
S.10.3.8			also expended. At S.1.0.3.8 the house was hit up. The Bosch was issued to cease firing. In all 86 rounds were fired. In the afternoon with T. Staff the attached the fronted Chequ. A very successful shoot, having been established got a first of our trenches. About 100 rounds were fired.	

Army Form C. 2118.

WAR DIARY
or
INTELLIGENCE SUMMARY.
(Erase heading not required.)

Instructions regarding War Diaries and Intelligence Summaries are contained in F. S. Regs., Part II. and the Staff Manual respectively. Title pages will be prepared in manuscript.

Place	Date	Hour	Summary of Events and Information	Remarks and references to Appendices
	18th		Throughout the day, there was little or no firing. Not open fire. Enemy shot in Yhaven, damage to gun pits &c.	
	19th	9pm	Intermittent firing throughout the day. At night an enemy motor with two guns on our left, we fired for five minutes from 9.40 to 9.50 pm. We fired 30 rounds.	
	20th		We did not fire throughout the day. Two new emplacements were noticed in Highland Street.	
	21st		A few rounds were fired to try & dislodge &. There were any of the enemy still hiding in shell holes. No movement was observed. Old firing on the enemy were now beyond range.	
	22nd			
	23rd		No firing the day was spent in the improvement of gun emplacements & ammunition recesses.	
X.6.0.3.8	24th		During the day little or no firing. At night we fired a few rounds at suspected firing point at Y.6.9.3.E	
X.6.0.1.8	25th		No firing during the day. At night 30 rounds were fired at X.6.0.3.E	
	26th		Intermittent firing in the forenoon on strong point X.6.0.3.E	

T2134. Wt. W708—776. 500000. 4/15. Sir J. C. & S.

Army Form C. 2118.

WAR DIARY
or
INTELLIGENCE SUMMARY.
(Erase heading not required.)

Instructions regarding War Diaries and Intelligence Summaries are contained in F. S. Regs., Part II. and the Staff Manual respectively. Title pages will be prepared in manuscript.

Place	Date	Hour	Summary of Events and Information	Remarks and references to Appendices
X6.0.38	26"		Had camp on farm hill occupied	
	27"		Battery not firing; day spent in the improvement of road & ammunition dumps &c.	
	28"		Intermittent firing throughout the day	
E.8.6.6	29"		Relieved 110 T.P Brigade R.G.A. The Battery moved to pt E.8.6.6	
E.8.A 76	30"		In advance were 44" Syp. W. 2nd Cdn. Bde. old Battery moved to E.8.A 76.	

www.ingramcontent.com/pod-product-compliance
Lightning Source LLC
Chambersburg PA
CBHW081502160426
43193CB00014B/2565